SMARTEST AND silliest

Written by
Camilla de la Bédoyère

QEB Publishing

Designed and edited by Starry Dog Books Ltd
Picture research: Starry Dog Books Ltd

Consultant: Dr Gerald Legg,
Booth Museum of Natural History,
Brighton

Published in the United States by
QEB Publishing, Inc.
3 Wrigley, Suite A
Irvine, CA 92618

www.qed-publishing.co.uk

Library of Congress Cataloging-in-Publication
Data
De la Bédoyère, Camilla.
  Smartest and silliest / Camilla de la Bédoyère.
    p. cm. -- (QEB Animal opposites)
  Includes index.
  ISBN 978-1-59566-761-8 (library binding)
  1. Animal intelligence--Juvenile literature. 2.
Animals--Juvenile literature. I. Title.
    QL785.D35 2011
    590--dc22
      2010010664

Printed in China

Picture credits
Key: t = top, b = bottom, l = left, r = right, c = centre,
FC = front cover, BC = back cover.

A = Alamy, BSP = Big Stock Photo.com, C = Corbis,
D = Dreamstime.com, F = Fotolibra.com,
FLPA = Frank Lane Picture Agency, G = Getty Images,
ISP = iStockphoto.com, M = Morguefile.com,
NPL = Nature Picture Library (naturepl.com),
PL = Photolibrary, PS = Photoshot,
S = Shutterstock.com, SPL = Science Photo Library.

FC t S/ © Timy, FC b S/ © Michael Rubin; BC l, tr, br
S/ © Picsfive, BC c S/ © fivespots.

1l S/ © Martin Spurny, 1r S/ © Francis Bossé;
2 S/ © Four Oaks; 3 S/ © Jens Stolt; 4 S/ © Four
Oaks; 5t PL/ © Jeanne Drake, 5b S/ © Four Oaks;
6c IQM/ © Masa Ushioda, 6-7 S/ © Jeffrey Van
Daele, 7t S/ © Gualtiero Boffi, 7c S/ © Francis
Bossé; 8c S/ © John A. Anderson, 8b S/ © Heiko
Kiera; 9t S/ © Cigdem Cooper, 9b IQM/ © Andre
Seale; 10bl A/ © David Hosking, 10-11 NHPA/PS
© Anthony Bannister; 11tr PL/ © Bildagentur
RM, 11bl PL/ © Reinhard Dirscherl, 11br S/ ©
AMA; 12t S/ © Dwight Smith, 12b PL/ © Tsuneo
Nakamura; 13 S/ © Leonid Smirnov; 14t © Stephen
P. Yanoviak, 14b S/ © Horia Bogdan; 15t S/ © Jens
Stolt, 15b FLPA/ © Konrad Wothe; 16 NPL/ © Doc
White; 17t © Ewa Krzyszczyk, c/o Georgetown
University, 17b NPL/ © Premaphotos; 18t S/ ©
Helen E. Grose, 18b © The Alex Foundation;
19t S/ © Hordlena, 19b S/ © Mlorenz; 20t
NPL/ © Andrew Murray, 20-21 PL/ © Juniors
Bildarchiv, 21t S/ © Richard Peterson; 22t PL/ ©
JW Alker, 22b NPL/ © Constantinos Petrinos;
23t © S/ Dennis Sabo, 23b © Otago Daily Times,
New Zealand; 24l S/ © Martin Spurny, 24r PL/
© Christie's Images; 25t S/ © Four Oaks, 25b
NPL/ © Simon King; 26c NPL/ © John Downer
Productions, 26b S/ © Steve Byland; 27t NPL/ ©
Nick Garbutt, 27b S/ © Dr Morley Read; 28bl NPL/
© Karl Ammann, 28-29 PL/ © Miriam Agron, 29b
S/ © Dudarev Mikhail; 32 S/ © Steve Byland.

The words in **bold**
are explained in
the glossary on
page 30.

Contents

Best Behavior

The way that an animal behaves is a clue to how smart it is. There are some super-smart animals, but others are not so brainy.

Elephants are extremely clever. When young elephants take a nap, their mothers stand over them to give them shade. As the sun moves across the sky, the elephants change their position, so the sleeping babies stay in the shade.

⇩ *Elephants have long childhoods, like humans. Their mothers teach them how to wash, find food, and stay safe.*

4

Tool users

Elephants doodle with sticks in the sand and use sticks to scratch their backs. They communicate with one another by making rumbling, trumpeting and other noises, and they have very long memories. Sometimes, elephants help sick, or injured members of their family.

⇦ *African elephants use their tusks to strip bark from trees. They eat the bark, or use it to swat flies.*

ACTUAL «« SIZE »»

Dung beetle

No one teaches dung beetles how to behave—they know by **instinct**. These beetles roll elephant dung into balls and bury it as food for their **grubs**. On a busy night, one beetle can bury 25 times its own weight in dung!

in   1   2   3

Brain Power

The ability to learn can give some animals an advantage.

Animals that learn new ways to behave have a better chance of surviving than those that make the same mistakes again and again.

What is a brain?

A brain is a collection of nerve cells, called neurons. Intelligent animals have more neurons than less clever ones. The neurons can connect to each other in lots of different ways. Animals with **complex brains** are better at learning and remembering, but this takes energy, so they have to eat plenty of food.

The no. 1 heaviest brain **RECORD BREAKER** is the ...

SPERM WHALE

The sperm whale has the heaviest brain of any animal. Its brain weighs about 18 pounds (8 kilograms). A human brain, by contrast, weighs just 3.1 pounds (1.4 kilograms). But this doesn't mean that sperm whales are brighter than us, because cleverness is about how a brain works, not just how big it is.

ACTUAL «« SIZE »»

Fish are not considered clever, but scientists have found that mosquito fish can count up to four!

Mosquito fish

⬇ Frogs are **amphibians**. This group of animals is not particularly smart, but wood frogs can learn which food tastes bad, and to avoid it.

Smart frogs

Wood frogs eat caterpillars because their instinct tells them that caterpillars are food. When a frog bites a hairy caterpillar, it discovers that it tastes bad and spits it out. After trying a handful of hairy caterpillars, the frog learns to avoid them.

7

⬇ Sheep may not look smart, but they learn how to recognize each other's faces. They can learn up to 50 sheep faces, which all look much the same to us!

Simple Solutions

⇨ *Instinct helps green turtles find their way in the open sea.*

All animals rely on instinct as well as **intelligence**.

Animals have instincts, which are the rules for behavior that they are born with. Butterflies, for example, have an instinct to fly to colorful flowers to find sweet **nectar** to drink.

Head for the sea

When baby turtles hatch from their eggs, they head straight for the sea, and swim to their feeding grounds far away. When it is time for the females to lay their own eggs, they instinctively find their way back to the same beach where they hatched.

The no. 1 butterfly migration **RECORD BREAKER** is the ...

MONARCH BUTTERFLY

One female monarch butterfly flew an amazing 1864 miles (3000 kilometers) in a single year. Monarch butterflies fly to warmer places to survive the winter. Instinct tells them to make this journey.

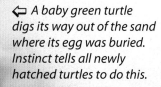

⇦ *A baby green turtle digs its way out of the sand where its egg was buried. Instinct tells all newly hatched turtles to do this.*

Olive ridley turtles are just 2.8 inches (7 centimeters) long when they hatch and embark on their incredible journeys. They can swim for hundreds, or even thousands, of miles a year.

ACTUAL «« SIZE »»

Olive ridley turtle

Turtle know-how

The turtles begin life knowing how to find their way to the sea and the way back to their beach. They may use the Earth's magnetic field and ocean currents to do this. They may also remember parts of their outward journey.

in 1 2

Working Lunch

Smart animals use their brain power to find food.

Honey badgers are one of the most fearless of all African animals. They hunt almost anything, including **venomous** snakes and crocodiles.

Honey-lovers

The favorite food of the honey badger, however, can be found inside a well-hidden bees' nest. Honey badgers have learned that honeyguide birds often perch near the hidden nests.

⇨ *Honey badgers climb trees in search of bees' nests.*

Smart birds

Once the birds have shown the badgers where the bees are, they sit and wait while the badgers do the hard job of ripping open the nest. Both animals then tuck in to a feast of honey and grubs.

⇦ *Honeyguide birds live in Africa and Asia, in forests, grasslands, and gardens.*

As many as six pale chanting goshawks follow one honey badger at a time.

The no. 1 least fussy eater **RECORD BREAKER** is the ...

TIGER SHARK

Tiger sharks are one of the world's least fussy eaters and are sometimes known as 'rubbish bins with fins'. They eat whatever they see, including their own babies. They have even swallowed car tires!

Hungry hawks

Following behind the honey badgers are hungry goshawks. These birds of prey fly high above the badgers and wait for them to dig for food. Then they swoop down to catch any rats or lizards that escape.

11

Grass-eating animals, such as cows, do not need smart feeding tactics. They can just spend all day grazing on the grass that is all around them.

Watch Out!

Animals that live by instinct can end up in tricky situations.

Clever creatures are able to teach their young how to avoid danger because they have learned from experience. Survival can be tough if you are not so smart.

Marching crabs

Every year, about 47 million red crabs on Christmas Island (a territory of Australia) march from their rainforest home to the sea. They need to get to the sea to mate. Instinct tells the crabs which way to walk, but it does not help them learn how to cross roads safely. Thousands get run over every year.

Grunt fish

ACTUAL «« SIZE »»»

Grunt fish can teach each other where to find food. Each group of fish has a teacher, whose job it is to show young fish, and ones that have just joined the group, where the best feeding grounds are.

⇦ After mating, the male red crabs walk to the rainforest. The females return later, after they have released their eggs into the sea.

Dodgy diets

Pandas are close to **extinction**. One reason for this is their choice of food. These bears eat bamboo, and not much else. Most of the bamboo passes through their bodies **undigested**. After many years, all the bamboo in one area may die off, and the pandas that live there starve to death.

⇩ *Every day, a giant panda has to seek out bamboo to eat. It spends about 13 hours eating up to 84 pounds (38 kilograms) of bamboo.*

For the Family

When animals reproduce, they mate and have young. Reproduction is a basic instinct.

While all animals have the instinct to reproduce, some of them use their intelligence to get the best mates.

⇧ The end of the ant's body is swollen and red, to resemble a tasty, tempting berry.

The no. 1 bravest mate **RECORD BREAKER** is the ...

PRAYING MANTIS

Male praying mantids are either the bravest animals, or the dimmest! During mating, they risk getting eaten by their mate. This male has had a lucky escape—the female is snacking on a dragonfly instead!

Red alert!

Tiny worms living inside the bodies of ants turn the ants' bodies red. This tricks birds into thinking the ants are tasty berries. When a bird gobbles up one of these ants, the worm eggs pass through the bird and end up in its **feces.** Ants eat the eggs when they eat the feces. The eggs then hatch and the whole cycle begins again.

Beautiful bowers

A female bowerbird chooses to mate with the male that has built the best **bower** from twigs and leaves. The bower is where mating takes place. Each male chooses how to decorate his bower. He may use shiny plastic, coins, flowers or berries. Some birds even have a favourite color!

ACTUAL «« SIZE »»»

Emperor moth

Male emperor moths use their feathery antennae to find females. They can detect one tiny particle of a pheromone—a chemical signal made by the females—7 miles (11 kilometers) away, and follow the scent to find her.

⇩ *This male gardener bird has put a lot of time and effort into building his bower. He has chosen blue decorations to attract a mate.*

15

That's Handy

The ability to use tools can be a sign of intelligence.

Intelligent animals find ways to solve problems. One way to tackle a problem is to use a tool to help you—especially when it comes to getting food.

⇩ *Sea otters often have a favorite stone, which they keep for a long time. This means they are thinking about the future.*

Using a hard surface

Shellfish are tough to break into. Sea otters lie on their back and balance a rock on their belly. Then they bash the shellfish against the rock until it cracks open. It may take 30 blows to open just one clam.

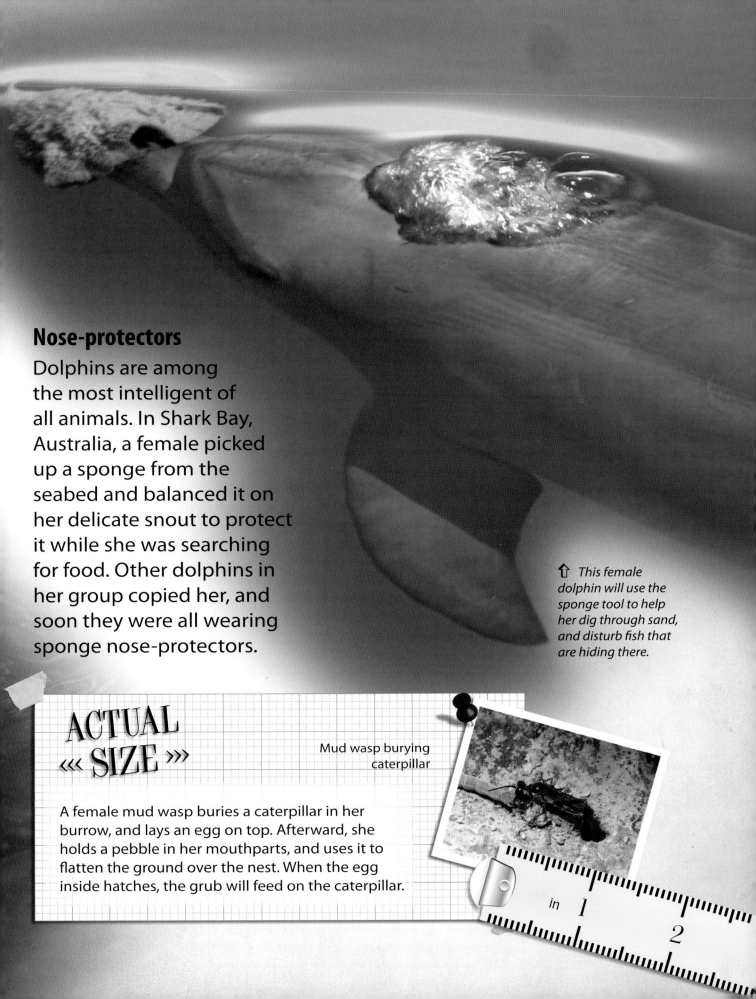

Nose-protectors

Dolphins are among the most intelligent of all animals. In Shark Bay, Australia, a female picked up a sponge from the seabed and balanced it on her delicate snout to protect it while she was searching for food. Other dolphins in her group copied her, and soon they were all wearing sponge nose-protectors.

⇧ *This female dolphin will use the sponge tool to help her dig through sand, and disturb fish that are hiding there.*

ACTUAL ⋘ SIZE ⋙

Mud wasp burying caterpillar

A female mud wasp buries a caterpillar in her burrow, and lays an egg on top. Afterward, she holds a pebble in her mouthparts, and uses it to flatten the ground over the nest. When the egg inside hatches, the grub will feed on the caterpillar.

in 1   2

All Talk

Intelligent animals can communicate with each other, and with us.

Less clever creatures are also able to send messages to each other, often noisily.

⇧ *When the male American bullfrog croaks, it fills its throat sac with air. Females prefer males with deeper voices, made by larger throat sacs.*

Croakers

Frogs and toads croak to attract females and to scare other males away. American bullfrogs are especially loud. Their croaks are amplified—made louder—by a big throat sac and a pair of vibrating **eardrums**.

Talking birds

Some birds are able to copy sounds, and are called mimics. Mynah birds are among the best bird mimics in the world. They can copy words and phrases, and even use different "voices" when they talk. Parrots, however, are even smarter and can be taught how to use words to express feelings, such as hunger.

The no. 1 cleverest talking bird **RECORD BREAKER** is ...

ALEX THE TALKING PARROT

Alex was a gray parrot who spent 30 years learning how to communicate with humans. When he died, Alex knew more than 100 words, could make up simple sentences and could count to six.

↓ *Hill mynahs are the best mimics of all. They live wild in Southern Asia, but many are kept as pets.*

ACTUAL ⟪ SIZE ⟫

Grasshopper

In summer, male grasshoppers rub their back legs against their wings to make loud chirping noises. The chirps tell other males to stay away, and also attract females. Beetles and spiders can rub body parts together to send messages, too.

19

Fast Learners

The brightest animals can learn new skills quickly.

Some animals may seem rather silly because of the way they behave, but they are smarter than they look!

Copy-cat apes

Orangutans are possibly the greatest copy-cats in the world. These big **apes** watch humans and copy their actions so quickly that they have learned to saw wood, hammer nails and even wash clothes with soap.

⇩ This orangutan has learned how to wash clothes. Orangutans live on the islands of Borneo and Sumatra, in South East Asia.

20

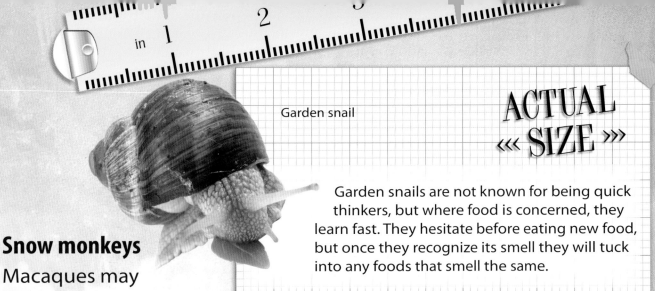

Garden snail

Garden snails are not known for being quick thinkers, but where food is concerned, they learn fast. They hesitate before eating new food, but once they recognize its smell they will tuck into any foods that smell the same.

Snow monkeys

Macaques may look daft sitting in steaming hot-water springs, but they have learned that this is a good way to keep warm when there is snow and ice about. They can also roll snowballs and even show one another how to make bigger, better ones.

⬇ *While some groups of Japanese macaques have learned to enjoy a soak in hot springs, others have learned how to wash their food.*

21

Underwater Wonders

Some of the simplest creatures live in the seas and oceans.

The underwater world is also home to some smart beasts that are surprisingly clever. Octopuses, for example, have impressive brain power.

Purple flatworm

ACTUAL ‹‹‹ SIZE ›››

Purple flatworms look pretty, but not smart. However, they do have simple brains. Not only can they find their way through mazes, but they can also remember the fastest route.

⇦ Veined octopuses have learned that they can hide inside shells and coconut husks. They carry the shells around with them, and climb inside when they need protection.

Sponges

Sponges are the simplest of animals—they have no intelligence at all! They not only lack brains—they don't even have any neurons (nerve cells). In fact, they are little more than tubes that can feed, breathe and reproduce.

⇧ *Tube sponges may be simple, but they are often colorful and can be over 3 feet (1 meter) tall.*

Eight-armed wonders

Small octopuses hide in empty shells to avoid predators, and larger ones can use their **tentacles** to open jars and get at food inside. Octopuses are the most intelligent of all invertebrates (animals without backbones).

The no. 1 sneakiest octopus **RECORD BREAKER** is...

SID THE OCTOPUS

One smart captive octopus named Sid used to sneak out of his tank every night. He climbed into nearby tanks to eat the fish, then went back to his own tank. Only a trail of water gave him away!

23

Memory Marvels

Brains are able to remember things. Without a memory, it would not be possible to learn.

There are different types of memory: remembering how to do things, remembering events, and remembering facts.

Bird brains

Pigeons have proved that they can learn to recognize different painting styles. After being shown lots of paintings by the artists **Picasso** and **Monet**, a group of pigeons were shown a painting they had never seen before, and were able to identify which of these two artists had painted it. Their memories helped them to learn the different styles.

⇩ *Picasso's paintings often have bold colors and shapes.*

⇧ *Pigeons can remember how places look and smell. This helps them find their way home.*

Tanks for the memories

It is often said that goldfish keep memories for just three seconds. A schoolboy, however, proved that they have longer memories. He taught his fish to find food next to a red plastic brick. Every day, the fish went to the brick to look for its food. Then the boy took the brick away. A few days later, he put the brick back in a different place, and the goldfish swam straight to it!

⇧ *A good memory might help a goldfish remember where to find food.*

The no. 1 longest memory **RECORD BREAKER** is the ...

ELEPHANT

Elephants can remember their dead friends and relatives for longer than any other animal, except humans. They return to the places where members of their group died, even years later, to mourn.

Would You Believe It?

Even smart animals sometimes do strange or silly things.

Creatures often look crazy or funny to us—but they have good reasons for the way they act and look.

Oops, I did it again!

Western fence lizards are not "bright sparks" when it comes to climbing. They chase their prey with such enthusiasm that they often fall out of trees. Males are particularly clumsy, falling when they are trying to show off to their mates. Most of the time, they pick themselves up and run straight back up the tree.

➡ *Western fence lizards are also called blue-bellies. Males have this blue coloring, but females are plain.*

The no. 1 smelliest animal **RECORD BREAKER** is the ... **SPOTTED SKUNK**

Skunks use a foul-smelling liquid called musk to send their attackers running. They give a warning signal first—by doing a handstand! If this isn't enough to scare off their attacker, they release the musk from their bottom and spray it at their attacker's face.

Big nose

The funny-looking
proboscis monkey
looks dim-witted,
but it is a clever
creature—except
when it leaps. Its
nose can grow
so big that it
sometimes flips up
and hits the monkey
in the eye!

⇨ *Male proboscis
monkeys use their nose to
make loud calls. Each call
sounds like "kee-honk."*

27

ACTUAL
«« SIZE »»

Many beetles cannot turn themselves
over if they land upside down, so they
die. Click beetles, however, arch their
backs, leap 12 inches (30 centimeters)
into the air and flick their bodies over so
they land the right way up!

Click
beetle

in 1   2   3

Monkeying Around

Monkeys, apes and their close relatives, humans, are the smartest animals.

Chimpanzees live in family groups, form friendships, and even teach one another how to do new things.

Tools for the job

Chimps use leaves to soak up water from tree hollows, and sticks to pull **termites** out of their mounds. They throw stones at leopards to scare them away, and use rocks to smash open nuts.

⇨ *Chimps use sounds, such as grunts and shrieks, to communicate. They also hug, kiss, and stroke each other.*

⇦ *This chimp learned how to use a tool by watching and copying its mother.*

28

Signs and symbols

Chimps can communicate with one another, and scientists have been able to teach them how to use sign language, recognize symbols, and do simple math. It is possible that a chimp is even able to imagine what another chimp is thinking.

The no. 1
silliest animal
**RECORD
BREAKER** is the ...

HUMAN

Humans are the most intelligent of all
animals on the planet. Yet they are also
the only animals that have been able
to cause massive damage to their own
environment—so they also qualify as the
silliest animals of all.

Glossary

Amphibian Frogs, toads and newts are amphibians. They lay their eggs in water.

Ape Apes are related to monkeys, but do not have tails. Gorillas, chimps and orangutans are apes.

Bower A private space used by a male to attract a female.

Complex brain Intelligent animals have brains that are described as complex.

Eardrum Sound waves enter an ear and hit the eardrum, which vibrates. The brain interprets these vibrations as sounds.

Extinction This is the process of becoming extinct, when all the animals of a particular type, or species, have died out.

Feces The solid waste that an animal produces.

Grub A young insect, especially a beetle, is called a grub.

Instinct A type of behavior that an animal is born with.

Intelligence Intelligent animals can solve problems and learn how to do new things. They have, or show, intelligence.

Monet Claude Monet (1840 – 1926) was a great French artist.

Nectar This is the sugary juice made by flowers.

Picasso Pablo Picasso (1881 – 1973) was a great artist and sculptor from Spain.

Tentacle A long, thin, flexible limb used for grabbing, moving or sensing things.

Termite An insect that looks like an ant and lives in groups of up to one million.

Undigested Food that passes through the body without being broken down is undigested.

Venomous Animals that produce a poisonous liquid, or venom, are described as venomous.

Index

31

Notes for Parents and Teachers

Here are some ideas for activities that adults and children can do together.

◆ Go through the book together and find examples of animals that learn how to do new things.

◆ Talk about the differences between humans and other animals. Ask the child to write a list of things that most animals and humans do, such as eat or move, and then write a list of things that people can do, but animals can't.

◆ Ask children what new skills they would like to learn (diving or knitting, for example). Ask them to think about what they would need to have or know to be able to learn that skill, how much time and hard work it would require and what the rewards might be.

◆ Hang a birdfeeder where children can see the birds feeding. Teach them how to watch wildlife without disturbing it, to record which types of birds visit the birdfeeder and to watch the way they feed.

◆ Children can witness smart animals in the world about them. Those with pets can share stories of their clever animals. Zoos and wildlife parks are good places to watch monkeys and apes.

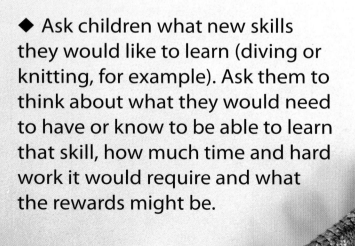